21st Century Skills INNOVATION *Library*

From Termite Den to ...
Office Building

by Nel Yomtov

Published in the United States of America by Cherry Lake Publishing
Ann Arbor, Michigan
www.cherrylakepublishing.com

Content Adviser: Marjan Eggermont, Senior Instructor, Schulich School of Engineering, Calgary, Alberta, Canada

Reading Adviser: Marla Conn, ReadAbility, Inc.

Design: The Design Lab

Photo Credits: Cover and page 3, ©Ken Wilson-Max/Alamy; cover inset and page 10, ©Piotr Gatlik/ Shutterstock, Inc.; page 4, ©Anton Chalakov/Shutterstock, Inc.; page 6, ©Realchemyst/Shutterstock, Inc.; page 7, ©Aleksey Stemmer/Shutterstock, Inc.; page 9, ©smuay/Shutterstock, Inc.; page 13, ©Jay Hocking/ Shutterstock, Inc.; page 14, damien_farrell / http://www.flickr.com / CC BY 2.0; page 16, ©Craig Buchanan/ Alamy; page 17, garybembridge / http://www.flickr.com / CC BY 2.0; page 20, ©kzww/Shutterstock, Inc.; page 21, ©Artazum and Iriana Shiyan/Shutterstock, Inc.; page 23, ©Dmitriy Komarov/Shutterstock, Inc.; page 25, ©AP Photo/Koji Sasahara; page 27, ©deadlyphoto.com/Alamy; page 29, ©Bettmann/Corbis / AP Images.

Library of Congress Cataloging-in-Publication Data
Yomtov, Nelson.
 From termite den to . . . office building / by Nel Yomtov.
    pages cm. – (Innovations from nature)
 Includes bibliographical references and index.
 ISBN 978-1-62431-755-2 (library binding) – ISBN 978-1-62431-767-5 (pdf) –
ISBN 978-1-62431-761-3 (paperback) – ISBN 978-1-62431-773-6 (e-book)
 1. Office buildings–Design and construction–Juvenile literature. 2. Architecture–Technological innovations–Juvenile literature. 3. Termites–Habitations–Juvenile literature. 4. Biomimicry– Juvenile literature. I. Title.
 NA6230.Y65 2014
 720–dc23   2013031285

Cherry Lake Publishing would like to acknowledge the work of
The Partnership for 21st Century Skills.
Please visit www.p21.org for more information.

Printed in the United States of America
Corporate Graphics Inc.
January 2014

CONTENTS

CHAPTER ONE

Modern Comforts

Even when a mall is crowded with people on a hot day, the air inside is usually cool.

Have you ever wondered how the temperature in a mall, a movie theater, or a large office building seems just right? When it's hot outside, it's usually nice and cool inside. When it's cold outside, you're warm and toasty inside. The temperatures in a modern building are controlled by a heating and cooling system. The cooling system is commonly known as air-conditioning.

The first modern air-conditioning system was developed in 1902. The owners of the Sackett-Wilhelms Lithographing and Publishing Company in Brooklyn, New York, were having a problem with **humidity** at their plant. The paper absorbed moisture from the hot summer air. This made it difficult to apply inks to the paper. A young electrical **engineer** named Willis Haviland Carrier came up with an idea to solve the problem. Carrier set up a system of chilled pipes and passed the air inside the building over them. The air cooled as it passed over the pipes. Because cool air doesn't hold as much moisture as warm air, the humidity in the plant was reduced. As a result, the paper stayed dry enough to use.

Modern heating and cooling systems are far more complex than Carrier's concept. They require many parts to operate smoothly. Some buildings require more than one system. Although many parts of the system are huge, you may never see any of them. They are often placed in ceilings, on rooftops, or in basements.

A modern cooling system uses chilled water to cool the air. The chilled water is pumped to a machine located in an **air duct**. The air duct is often hidden in the ceiling. Air passes through the duct and cools down as it moves past the machine. The chilled air travels through the duct. It escapes through vents into stores, offices, and other open spaces.

6

The heating side of the system also uses water. A water boiler is used to create steam or heated water. The steam or water is then pumped to a heat exchanger inside the air duct. Air is warmed as it passes through the heat exchanger. The warm air escapes through vents into living spaces the same way cool air does.

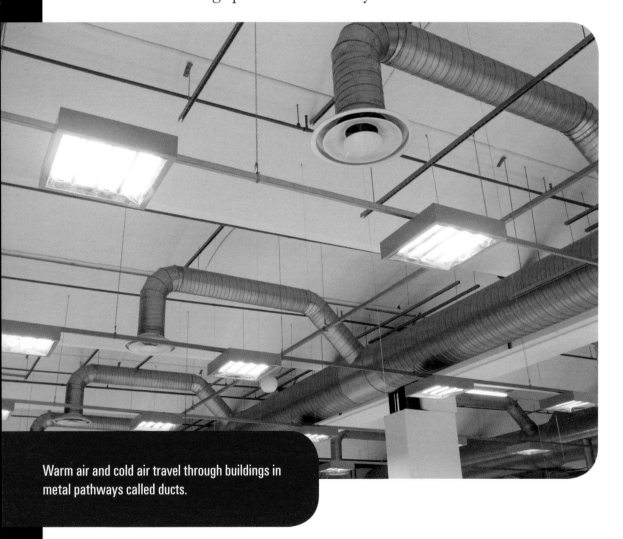

Warm air and cold air travel through buildings in metal pathways called ducts.

From Termite Den to . . . Office Building

Large buildings often have boiler systems that take up an entire room.

In a typical office building in the United States, heating and cooling account for about half of the building's total energy use. This makes those systems good targets for energy savings. Many offices cut down on heating and cooling costs by turning the systems down whenever possible. During hours when businesses are closed, offices often turn temperature settings down in cold weather and up in warm weather. Energy experts also urge building owners and tenants to regularly clean and maintain the heating and cooling systems.

Standard heating and cooling systems do a great job keeping us comfortable year-round. But they have some drawbacks. They are often very costly to install, maintain, and repair. They also require a huge amount of electricity to operate. As the cost of electricity rises, running these systems has become very expensive.

Engineers and **architects** are faced with solving these problems. They began to wonder how they could build modern structures with more efficient heating and cooling systems. Some building designers thought outside the box and turned to nature for the answer. They found the solution in a tiny, yet remarkable, insect—the termite.

CHAPTER TWO

Nature's Master Builders

Termites have thrived on Earth for more than 300 million years. They live in almost all parts of the world in huge numbers. Most of us think of termites only as destructive, wood-munching creatures that invade our homes. But there's more to these tiny insects than meets the eye.

Termites have a unique lifestyle. Many kinds of termites are difficult to locate because they live in

Though termites can cause problems for homeowners, they are impressive builders.

Large termite colonies are capable of building massive dens.

wood or underground. Others build mounds, or dens. These remarkable structures are shaped like cones, half circles, or towers. Many dens are taller than a person. To build the mounds, termites use their saliva and other body fluids to cement soil particles together. Then they slowly build their dens, particle by particle. The dens are incredibly strong. Many can even survive fires and floods.

Inside the den, termites dig tunnels, chambers, and even dead ends, where they often store their waste. Some termites dig special rooms where they grow a type of **fungi**. Termites supply the fungi with chewed wood fiber. The fungi break down the wood fiber into food for the termites.

Termites' building techniques allow them to control the temperature and humidity in their homes. The den serves and protects the termite colony's underground nest. Some nests can be as deep as 6 feet (1.8 meters) underground. In a sense, mound-building termites are themselves architects. They are masters of building structures that meet all of their needs. But how does air **circulate** in termite dens?

Some dens have no openings to the outside. These are called capped chimney mounds. The air in a capped chimney mound is warmed by the high temperature outside and the heat made by the activity of the termites inside. The warm air from the underground nest rises to

Termites live together in large groups called colonies. There can be hundreds of thousands of termites in a single den. The colonies are divided into smaller groups. Members of each group look different, and each one has a role to play in helping the colony thrive. The king and queen of the colony are called the reproductives. The queen lays eggs. Only the king and queen have eyes. The reproductives are darker than the rest of the termites in the colony. Soldiers defend the nest from invading ants and termites from other colonies. Soldiers have large heads and strong jaws. Workers build the den, gather food, and care for the young.

the mound's **porous** surface. There, the heat in the air passes through the porous walls to the outside. Fresh air drops back down into open spaces below the nest and then through the den again.

Dens that have vents to the outside are called open chimney mounds. The air in this type of mound circulates differently than in a capped chimney mound. The large opening at the top of the mound is exposed to higher wind speeds than openings near the ground. Fresh air is drawn into the mound through the lower openings. It passes upward through the nest until it finally flows out of the top opening.

In 2008, researchers J. Scott Turner and Rupert C. Soar published a paper that questioned these explanations of temperature control in termite dens. They claim dens operate in much more complex ways. More research is currently being conducted to get to the bottom of the debate.

Mick Pearce is an architect who was born in the African nation of Zimbabwe. He has lived and worked in Australia, England, and Zambia, in southern Africa. Pearce wants to design buildings with low maintenance costs and **renewable energy** systems. He also wants his designs to draw inspiration from local nature. Using nature as a model is called **biomimicry**. Biomimicry is a field that studies nature and copies its forms and systems to solve human problems. Pearce has drawn inspiration from the mound-building termites of his homeland.

Some termite dens are shaped like giant mushrooms.

CHAPTER THREE

How It's Done

Eastgate Center is one of Zimbabwe's most unusual buildings.

In 1992, Mick Pearce was hired to design the Eastgate Center in Harare, Zimbabwe. The building is Zimbabwe's largest office and shopping center. It covers half a city block in the business center of Harare. It opened in 1996. Pearce based his design for Eastgate on the termite mounds he had observed since he was a young boy. The building is a groundbreaking achievement.

Pearce realized that termites had accomplished something remarkable. In southern Africa, they can only survive if their dens maintain a temperature of 86 to 88 degrees Fahrenheit (30 to 31 degrees Celsius). As temperatures in Zimbabwe swing from a chilly 54°F (12°C) at night to a steamy 95°F (35°C) during the day, the termites must work hard to survive. Throughout the day, they dig vents at the bottom of open chimney mounds. This cools the air and sends hot air out through the top vent. All day long, they open up new tunnels and block others to control the heat and humidity inside the den.

Pearce was just as clever with the Eastgate Center. He designed two buildings side by side with an open space in the center. The space between the buildings is covered in glass. The buildings are made of concrete.

Pearce based his plans on a concept called passive cooling. It works by storing heat in the day and venting it at night as temperatures drop. At the start of the day, the buildings are cool. During the day, temperatures increase as the sun shines and people and machines create heat, which rises upward. The concrete buildings absorb and store the heat for later use. The temperature inside increases only slightly.

In the evening, the temperature outside drops. Large fans are used to draw the stored heat out from the concrete walls. This "empties" the walls and gets them ready to receive a new load of heat the next day. Fans also draw in cool air at the bottom of the building, like the vents that termites open at the bottom of their dens. This air takes the place of the warmer daytime air. The warmer air is sent out through a series of giant chimneys at the top of the building. These chimneys are like the

Portcullis House, in London, England, uses a heating and cooling system based on the one used in Eastgate Center.

Mick Pearce's design helps keep the Eastgate Center at a comfortable temperature without using much energy.

Life & Career Skills

Planning and designing modern buildings and other structures can be an exciting career choice. There are many different skills involved in becoming a successful architect. Design, engineering, and communication skills are among the most important. Start preparing for your college degree by taking high school classes in English, physics, and math. To help sharpen your visual skills, try your hand at art courses. You could study drawing, sculpture, or photography. As an architecture student in college, you'll study writing, computer design, art history, and building construction. Most college grads work for several years as interns at an architectural firm. After that, they have to pass exams to receive a license to become a professional architect.

vents at the top of a termite mound. The cooled air is also stored and then directed by fans into offices through vents the next day.

Pearce's design uses the air ventilation processes seen in both capped chimney mounds and open chimney mounds. The heat from the people and machines in the buildings rise toward the rooftop just as warm air rises in a capped chimney mound. Eastgate's tall stacks of chimneys and lower-level fans serve the same function as the top and bottom vents of an open chimney mound.

Pearce's innovations led to some impressive results. The Eastgate Center **ventilates**, cools, and heats by natural methods. It also saves money. Its ventilation costs only 10 percent of a similar air-conditioned structure. It uses 35 percent less energy than six ordinary buildings. In its first five years, Eastgate saved more than $3.5 million in energy costs.

Pearce was just getting started. In the following years, he continued to improve the concepts he used at the Eastgate Center. His next big design was the Council House Two (CH2) in Melbourne, Australia, which opened in 2006. CH2 has shops on the ground floor and nine floors of offices above. At night, windows on one side of the building automatically open. This lets in the cool night air. The heat built up in the concrete walls and ceilings is removed by the cool air through windows on the other side of the building. Devices on the roof release warm air from individual floors through roof vents.

In the daytime, water is used to cool the air inside the building. The water is run down the outside of the building through five 43-foot (13 m) tubes, or "shower towers." The towers cool and **evaporate** the water, then direct it as cool air into the stores on the ground floor of the building. The remaining water is cooled again and pumped from the basement to chilled beams at every level of the building. The beams give off cool air later in the day after the effects of the nighttime cooling wear off.

As a result of Pearce's design, CH2 uses an estimated 80 percent less energy and 70 percent less water than a traditional building.

CHAPTER FOUR

Looking Ahead

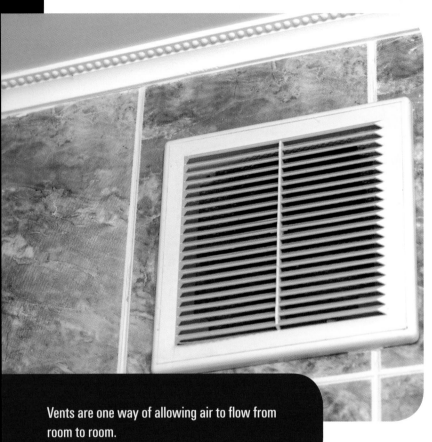

Vents are one way of allowing air to flow from room to room.

Walls are built to separate spaces from one another. We build walls to separate schools and businesses from the outside world. Inside, we build walls to separate one classroom or office from others. After we've separated spaces from one another, we have to build other things to

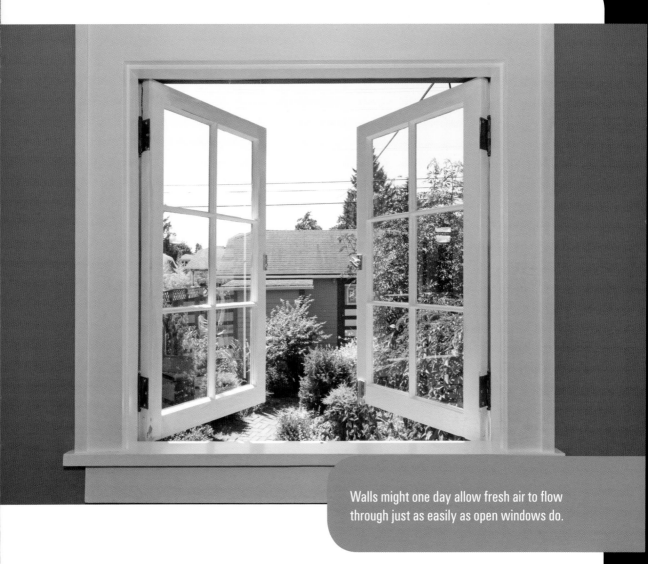

Walls might one day allow fresh air to flow through just as easily as open windows do.

connect them! Windows, fans, air ducts, and heating systems are things that we must build to move something from one space into another space.

What if walls were not just barriers, but also pathways for air to move? We should be able to figure out

21st Century Content

People don't often think about the many benefits of termites. Without them, however, our environment would look much different. As termites dig tunnels in the soil, they leave behind nutrients that enrich the earth. This helps plant life to grow. The plants provide food for other species. When termites abandon their dens or a colony dies off, their homes and nests often make great living spaces for other creatures. Also, termites are a source of food for birds, spiders, and other insects. In some parts of Australia and Africa, people eat termites because the insects are high in healthy protein and fat.

how to create that. After all, even termites did! The porous walls inside and outside a termite den allow air to pass through. Imagine if we could build porous walls that allow winds to flow through. We could ventilate entire buildings without having to open a window and be hit with a strong gust of wind!

Australia's "magnetic" termites might provide us with new building directions. These termites build dens that are shaped like tall, thin blades. They are narrowest at the top and bottom and gently curve out in the center. The dens generally lie in a north–south direction, so they are similar to compass needles. As a result, they are commonly called compass mounds.

Researchers believe that the shape and arrangement of the dens allows the termites inside to make the most of their environment. When the sun is low and temperatures are cool, the mound gets a large amount of sunlight to its

Compass mounds are built in a direction that controls how much sunlight hits the den.

sides. This provides heat to warm the nest. When the sun is overhead and at its strongest, the narrow blade receives little sunlight. This prevents the den from absorbing too much heat. Perhaps these odd-looking structures will give engineers and architects some fresh ideas about building spaces for humans to work and live in.

Termites are here to stay, and we should continue to learn from them. Perhaps the answers to many of humankind's problems will be found in this tiny insect's remarkable building abilities.

CHAPTER FIVE

A Building Dream Team

Toyo Ito (1941–) is a Japanese architect whose designs are often inspired by nature. He was born in Seoul, South Korea. He graduated from the University of Tokyo with a degree in architecture. One of his best-known designs is Mediatheque, a library and gallery in Sendai City, Japan. Ito designed a series of tubes based on the structure of seaweed found in the oceans. The gently swaying tubes help

Toyo Ito won the 2013 Pritzker Architecture Prize. Many people consider it the world's most prestigious architecture prize.

Life & Career Skills

Architecture is a fascinating field and one worth considering as a career choice. An architect is someone who designs buildings and other construction projects. Architects are required to exercise a high degree of creativity and innovative thinking. They are often highly paid. If you choose a career in architecture, you'll most likely be challenged to push your talents to their limit, and you will have the chance to make the world a better place through your hard work.

support the building and connect the floors. When a devastating earthquake struck Japan in March 2011, Mediatheque was one of the few buildings left standing in the area. Ito has also used honeycomb-shaped designs and snakelike designs in his buildings.

Mick Pearce (1938–) is a world-famous architect who was born in the African nation of Zimbabwe. He graduated from the Architectural Association School of Architecture in London, England, in 1962. Since the late 1980s, Pearce has focused on biomimicry. One of the goals of his style is to protect the environment. His best-known building is the Eastgate Center in Harare, Zimbabwe. He was inspired by the mound-building termites of southern Africa when he created Eastgate's system of temperature control. His design of the CH2 building in Melbourne, Australia, follows many of the same principles he used at Eastgate. It also features many

Mick Pearce's Council House 2, or CH2, is an environmentally friendly government building in Melbourne, Australia.

21st Century Content

 The word *biomimicry* comes from the Greek words *bios*, meaning "life," and *mimesis*, meaning "to imitate." Biologist Janine Benyus made the term *biomimicry* popular in her book *Biomimicry: Innovation Inspired by Nature*, which was published in 1997. She has helped establish two organizations to advance the study of biomimicry. In 1998, Benyus cofounded the Biomimicry Guild, a company that helps develop products based on nature. In 2005, she founded the Biomimicry Institute. This organization promotes biomimicry concepts and educates the public about creating a healthier planet. The Biomimicry Guild and Institute were combined into one program in 2010. Together, they are called Biomimicry 3.8. The "3.8" in the name refers to the more than 3.8 billion years that life has existed on Earth.

new environmentally friendly functions. In 2003, Pearce was honored for his innovations with a Prince Claus Award from the Netherlands. After working in China on passive cooling systems from 2009 to 2012, he returned to work in his home country.

Eero Saarinen (1910–1961) was an American architect born in Finland. He is known for designing buildings with sweeping, arching curves. These shapes are based largely on the flight of birds. The TWA Flight Center at John F. Kennedy International Airport in New York City is one of his most famous designs. The building resembles the shape of a bird with outstretched, swooping wings. It was designated a historic landmark by the city and is also listed on the U.S. National Register of Historic Places.

Eero Saarinen designed some of the world's most famous buildings.

Glossary

air duct (AIR DUHKT) a structure that carries air from one place to another

architects (AHR-kuh-tekts) people who design buildings and supervise the way they are built

biomimicry (bye-oh-MI-mi-kree) the practice of studying and copying nature's forms and systems to solve human problems

circulate (SUR-kyuh-late) to move in a pattern

engineer (en-juh-NIR) someone who is specially trained to design and build things

evaporate (i-VAP-uh-rate) to change into a vapor or gas

fungi (FUHN-gye) plantlike organisms that have no leaves, roots, flowers, or chlorophyll and grow on decaying matter or other plants

humidity (hyoo-MID-ut-ee) the amount of moisture in the air

porous (POR-uhs) full of tiny holes that let air or liquids pass through

renewable energy (ri-NOO-uh-buhl EN-ur-jee) power from sources that can never be used up, such as wind, tides, and sunlight

ventilates (VEN-tuh-lates) allows fresh air into a place and lets stale air out

For More Information

BOOKS

Gates, Phil. *Nature Got There First*. New York: Kingfisher, 2010.

Lee, Dora. *Biomimicry: Inventions Inspired by Nature*. Tonawanda, NY: Kids Can Press, 2011.

WEB SITES

Biomimicry 3.8
www.biomimicry.net
Check out the latest news on the science of biomimicry, with links to other sites as well as information about choosing a career in the field.

HowStuffWorks—How Termites Work
http://science.howstuffworks.com/zoology/insects-arachnids/termite.htm
Learn more about termite society, how termites build mounds, and what to do if termites invade your house.

Mick Pearce—Architect
www.mickpearce.com
Visit Mick Pearce's official Web site to view photos of Eastgate Center, CH2, and some of his other buildings.

Index

About the Author

Nel Yomtov is an award-winning author of nonfiction books and graphic novels for young readers. He lives in the New York City area.